I WAS BORN
Like this

BISHOP OTIS KENNER II

WestBow Press
A DIVISION OF THOMAS NELSON
& ZONDERVAN

Copyright © 2014 Bishop Otis Kenner II.

All rights reserved. No part of this book may be used or reproduced by any means, graphic, electronic, or mechanical, including photocopying, recording, taping or by any information storage retrieval system without the written permission of the publisher except in the case of brief quotations embodied in critical articles and reviews.

Scripture taken from the King James Version of the Bible.

WestBow Press books may be ordered through booksellers or by contacting:

WestBow Press
A Division of Thomas Nelson & Zondervan
1663 Liberty Drive
Bloomington, IN 47403
www.westbowpress.com
1 (866) 928-1240

Because of the dynamic nature of the Internet, any web addresses or links contained in this book may have changed since publication and may no longer be valid. The views expressed in this work are solely those of the author and do not necessarily reflect the views of the publisher, and the publisher hereby disclaims any responsibility for them.

ISBN: 978-1-4908-3345-3 (sc)
ISBN: 978-1-4908-3347-7 (hc)
ISBN: 978-1-4908-3346-0 (e)

Library of Congress Control Number: 2014906902

Printed in the United States of America.

WestBow Press rev. date: 04/18/2014

Contents

Preface ix
Chapter 1:   The Inherent Condition 1
Chapter 2:   Disqualified by Association 7
Chapter 3:   Living through the Process of a
                    Mishandled Life 11
Chapter 4:   Living Life out Of Bounds 17
Chapter 5:   Civil War 23
Chapter 6:   The Practical Dilemma 31
Chapter 7:   Demonic Attendance 35
Chapter 8:   Repeat Offender 45
Chapter 9:   Attempt to Abort the Next Great Thing 51
Chapter 10: The Aftermath 65
Chapter 11: Counting Up the Cost 77
Chapter 12: I Survived 85
Chapter 13: Why Now? 91

Dedication

To Tyra Kenner, my beautiful wife of nearly nineteen years, and my mother, Gloria Blue Lee, for her support of and dedication to my ministry.

To the late Otis Kenner, Sr. and the late Martin Luther Lee, Sr., who supported me and helped me to develop into the man of God that I am.

To my ten beautiful children and their spouses and my seven wonderful grandchildren.

To my fourteen siblings, who were a part of my development and ministry.

To my best friend and pastor, Curtis and Sang Stacey.

To my beloved in the Lord, Rev. Dr. Albert Bailey.

To all the members of Fresh Faith Worship Center, both east and west bank locations.

And to the students of the River Region Theological College. I love you all.

Preface

This book is a must-read for every person who knows or feels as if he or she is dealing with a "pre-existing condition" like homosexuality, lesbianism, fornication, adultery, bisexuality, transgender personality, psychopathy, or addiction. Many homosexuals, transgender persons, and others listed above have asserted that they were "born like that." I agree, and I can prove the validity of their claim. One of the struggles that has captivated the twenty-first century is the struggle of sexual identity. Many people have been traumatized in some way by something or someone, resulting in finding themselves facing a truth about themselves that has either been openly expressed or shamefully hidden. As a result, their lives have been shipwrecked, and they are aimlessly wondering to find true purpose and identity.

Perhaps you are a parent who is helplessly watching your children take a downward spiral, displaying behavior problems, sexual promiscuity, or addictive behavior related to drugs and/or alcohol, and you are unsure why they are exhibiting such behavior. The truth may be that they've been sexually or mentally abused or that they are in a sexual identity crisis. This book is a perfect starting point to stimulate conversation. Let these words do the talking and bring your loved ones to a place of freedom and liberty through Christ Jesus. It can be the catalyst to a new beginning.

As you examine the contents of this book, you will find that the problem with mankind's sinful nature started long before we were born. I want to ease the pain of what most people cannot explain—how one can be born with sexual tendencies, whether heterosexual, homosexual, or other behaviors, whether addictive or inhumane—but know that what he or she is dealing with is not the result of a decision he or she made one morning, nor is it an assignment that was intellectually chosen. We make decisions in life, but rarely do we make them to accommodate temptations that dominated our lives before we really understood what they represented and the damage thy may cause. In fact, yes, I believe that many were born with a predisposition to certain sexual inclinations.

After his fall with Bathsheba, David said, "Behold, I was shapen in iniquity: and in sin did my mother conceive me"(Psalm 51:5 KJV). We are told religiously that we were born *in* sin, but we are not *with* sin, but the truth is that we were born both with sin and in sin. David realized that what he had done was not something that he signed up for but something that, in fact, signed *him* up! I want to expose the true origin of our behaviors, where they originated, and why even young children exhibit innate behaviors that no one taught them and that they did not learn. It is my mission to show the people who were born with tendencies to commit certain acts in life to understand that they can find the hope they need to break through this difficulty, understand their God-given identities and pursue their live without question about what God intended them to be. This book is filled with practical and heart-wrenching testimonies that can easily be applied to people in all walks of life.

CHAPTER 1

The Inherent Condition

> Wherefore, as by one man, sin entered into the world, and death by sin; and so death passed upon all men, for that all have sinned.
> —Romans 5:12 (KJV)

Adam put every person at a disadvantage through his transgression in the garden, and because we are the descendants of Adam, we have an *inherent condition*. "Inherent" is defined in the *American Heritage Student Dictionary* as being part of the basic nature of a person or thing. Adam's transgression opened a door in every person's life. Therefore, humankind, through human nature, became contaminated with the propensity for sin. As a result, every sin imaginable became an enticement to the flesh. By the laws of nature and of procreation, we inherently are products of that from which we came.

When Adam ate the forbidden fruit, he became conscious of every sin imaginable. His life was the seed, and the seed yielded after its kind.

> And God said, let the earth bring forth grass, the herb yielding seed, and the fruit tree yielding fruit after his kind whose seed in itself, upon the earth and it was so. (Genesis 1:11 KJV)

Everything God created has the ability to procreate. Not doing so is outside of its purpose. Hence, we encounter this inherent condition.

> For when we were in the flesh, the motion of sins, which were by the law did work in our members to bring forth fruit unto death. (Romans 7:5 KJV)

Consider the phrase, "motion of sin." A motion is a movement, arousal, attraction, or passion that works through the physical aspect of our being. The "motion of sin" is subtle, cunning, and deceitful. The moment we recognize that something is forbidden by law, there is another natural law, our inherent condition, pushing us to do it: the motion of sin. It may be surprising to discover that sin has a motion.

There is an inborn tendency to commit certain behaviors that are socially, emotionally, and religiously unacceptable, yet they are inevitable. We are of the basic nature of Adam. When we accept this fact, we can see how one can be born a homosexual, a lesbian, a fornicator, a liar, or a thief. Even though we were not taught these behaviors, it is without question that these spirits or tendencies were attached to us from early childhood.

Through religion we are taught to circumvent this inescapable truth, as if God needed a defense, but God is not at fault: the inherent condition of the basic human nature of Adam is at fault. We have created the saying that God created every person, when God did not, in fact, create every person. God created Adam and Eve, and every person was made their descendant. Adam was created in the image and after the likeness of God, but when he transgressed in the garden, he remained in the image of God but lost the likeness of God. All of his spiritual characteristics were compromised, and Adam died spiritually, meaning he was separated from God. Therefore, because we are the descendants of Adam, we were born spiritually dead, separated from God, with all kinds of sin and debauchery (unrestrained, self-indulgent, immoral behavior[1]). Therefore, our physical nature came from Adam, not from God. As Paul says, "For we know that the law is spiritual: but I am carnal sold under sin" (Romans 7:14 KJV).

To be "sold under sin" means that, through human nature, Adam sold every person out of the holiness required by God. This is why God the Father gave His Son to us: to give us His perfect nature, which is acceptable to God the Father. The first Adam sold us out, but the last Adam, Jesus Christ, bought us back by His blood and brings all those who receive Him through His blood back to the Father. This is redemption.

When David says, "Behold, I was shapen in iniquity; and in sin did my mother conceive me" (Psalm 51:5 KJV), he says he was "shapen" (or influenced, pushed, bent, pressured). In other words, life and one's environment can shape one into something that opposes one's true personality.

King David was on his rooftop when he should have been with his men in battle, and he saw Uriah's wife, Bathsheba, bathing on her rooftop. He sent for her and slept with her, and she conceived a child. King David had Uriah killed to conceal his—King David's—transgression. This is the same David who God said was one after His own heart who would do all His will (Acts 13:22).

---

[1] Encarta Dictionary

Therefore, we have to ask the question: Was David's behavior the heart of God? Certainly not. Rather, it's the inherent condition that opposes our true personality. David's example shows how a person can be called by God and be after God's heart yet live outside God's purpose for him or her.

For many of us, a single, tragic moment shaped, bent, and pushed us into a life that we inherently received from Adam. When I was a young child, some older male cousins molested me, gave me urine in an orange juice can to drink and a bumblebee in a cookie to eat, and afterward made fun of me and laughed at me. They were so much older. How could they do those things to me? I guess it was the inherent condition for them as well.

The bottom line is that the inherent condition causes injured people to injure other people. In retrospect, I know that I used control over women to conceal my pain, hurt, and shame. That single moment when I was a child shaped my life into one of lust and fornication. How did this happen? Look at what David said: "In sin did my mother conceive me." That inherent condition was already in me. Fornication was a seed passed through my spiritual DNA from one generation to the next until one day it showed up in me.

The inherent condition can manifest in many ways: drunkenness, hatred, drug use, murder, violence, bitterness, homosexuality, and so on. It sometimes lies dormant until something tragic happens that awakens that stagnated spirit, and when it finally comes alive, it manipulates, controls, and dominates its host's life.

We sometimes talk about generational curses in the church setting as if they affect only a select group of people, but the truth is that every person who was born of a woman and made after a man was born with the generational curse of Adam, called the Adamic nature. So yes, you were "born like that," but remember: the fault is not yours, nor is it God's; it is Adam's.

"Now then if I do that I would not, it is no more I that do it, but sin that dwelleth in me" (Romans 7:20 KJV), but I could also say, "It is the Adam in me." When one is born again through the Lord Jesus Christ, he or she receives another inherent condition, "holy, and unblamable and unreprovable in his sight" (Colossians 1:22 KJV).

CHAPTER 2

Disqualified by Association

Many believers today are trying to satisfy their religious convictions by "works of righteousness"—going to church, paying tithes, attending revivals, fasting, and praying—hoping that their actions will declare them holy and bury the struggles of a concealed life. Then they awaken from their dreams to discover they've fallen short again.

Adhering to church ethics and systems that are supposed to define you put you on a momentary high, but once your high subsides, you're back in the struggle again. There is a reason for our chase after this religious high: we are disqualified by association with Adam, as he has rendered every person's works unapproved by God: "But we are all as an unclean thing, and all our righteousness are as filthy rags (Isaiah 64:6 KJV).

There is a fault line bigger than the San Andreas that I call the *Adam*ic fault line. It runs through every human life, disqualifying us from being perfect in God by our association to Adam. If we are disqualified by our connection to Adam, why do we go through church ethics and regulations as a means of worship to God? Well, in this case, it's not a question of *what* you do. It's *why* you do what you do.

What We Do

If we think we can camouflage our lives by the service we render and thereby be acceptable to God, we are fooling ourselves. The fall of humankind presents our works contaminated, and we were void of the holiness required by God.

Why We Do What We Do

We do what we do to express our gratitude to God for having declared us "holy, unblameable, and unreprovable" (Colossians 1:22 KJV) in His sight through Jesus Christ, regardless of our past practices. However, in regard to our human efforts through the law and religious protocols, we are disqualified. According to Galatians 2:16 (KJV), "By the works of the law, no man shall be justified."

We must take note of this basic principle. If we don't qualify ourselves, when we fall short of His glory, we can't disqualify ourselves. We are not the qualifying factor. In other words, it was not our actions; nor our practices that declared us holy. It was Christ. Therefore, the believer never loses his/her placement because it was Christ who qualified us. If we stay under Adam, we are already disqualified no matter what we do.

> And be found in him, not having mine own righteousness, which is of the law, but that which is through the faith of Christ, the righteousness which is of God by Faith. (Philippians 3:9 KJV)

Adam brings into play every sin that a man is capable of committing when worship is offered outside of Christ, which renders the worship and the worshipper disqualified by association. However, we are only conditionally at fault and disqualified, but positionally in Christ, we are all accepted in the beloved. If we focus on our position in Christ, it will change our condition under Christ. Christ the Lord wants to trade places with you. He wants to take your place on the cross so you can take His place in the world. He has already met the civil, moral, spiritual, and religious criteria of holiness and acceptance with the Father; in other words, he took your test, and because he passed, you passed. Once you accept the Lord in your heart by faith, Christ becomes every person and every sin on the cross—fornicators, adulterers, homosexuals, lesbians, liars, murderers, addicts, and so on. He takes your place and qualifies you before God the Father.

We must pay special attention to the words in Scripture that are in past tense. Look at the words in this Scripture:

> To the praise of his glory of his grace wherein he hath made us accepted in the beloved.
> (Ephesians 1:6 KJV)

Hath, made, accepted, beloved: these words suggest that it is done already. Nothing is left for us to do but to receive it.

CHAPTER 3

Living through the Process of a Mishandled Life

And Jonathan, Saul's son, had a son that was lame of his feet. He was five years old when tidings came of Saul and Jonathan's out of Jazreel, and his nurse took him up, and fled: And it came to pass, as she made haste to flee, that he fell, and became lame and his name was Mephibosheth.

—2 Samuel 4:4 (KJV)

It was common for a king to kill off the sons of his predecessors so there could never be a legitimate claim to the throne. Although David did not approve of this behavior, Joab, the captain of his army, carried it out in spite of David's command not to. Mephibosheth, heir to the kingdom of Saul, was five years old when his nurse got the news. She lifted him up to run with him, but she dropped him, crippling him for life; it was she who Mephibosheth most trusted, his caregiver, she who nursed him, who dropped him. Mephibosheth's life was forever changed because the one he trusted mishandled his life.

Mephibosheth's injury was not the result of a self-inflicted wound but of someone else failing to do what she was entrusted to do. How many young girls have become prostitutes or lesbians or have turned to promiscuity because someone mishandled them? How many young boys have become homosexual or prostitutes or have turned to fornication because someone mishandled them? According to American Psychological Association, sixty percent of perpetrators of sexual abuse are known to the child but are not family members; thirty percent are family members and ten percent are strangers to the child. Many of you who are reading this book are living through the process of a mishandled life. Your actions are part of your process ... because *you've been dropped*! It may have been your aunt, uncle, brother, sister, cousin, mother, father, the man you mother brought home, or the woman your father brought home, but someone mishandled you; someone "dropped" you. Now your sexual identity is in confusion, and your lifestyle is the process of a mishandled life.

I wish I could tell you that when my older cousins molested me when I was five years old that that was the only time it happened, but it wasn't. When I was about thirteen years old, an elderly man who worked on junk cars lived next door, and I often went to his house and helped him. His daughter, who lived next door to him, had just bought her husband a new four-wheeler. I told her that it was a nice birthday present, and she told me that you are never too old for a birthday present; they just get bigger. Then she told me that, if I'd be her boyfriend, she'd buy me a big present just like the one she'd bought her husband. I could not respond to her indecent advances, so I made an excuse to leave and never returned until the day she died, when I went to pray for her. She mishandled me; she dropped me. The truth, as I found out later, was that she was a man who had changed his name to a woman's name, dressed like a woman, and unlawfully married another man.

I became psychologically crippled; I'd been dropped again and was confused after being mishandled. Depression, inferiority, and worthlessness staked a claim on my mental state, and I was too embarrassed to tell anyone because I was afraid of what others would think of me. It has taken me more than thirty-one years to speak about it. As I sit here writing, it's 4:46 am, and I am developing a migraine just thinking about that period in my life.

Let me explain what I meant when I referred to living through the process of a mishandled life. Like me, many of you experienced an event that changed the rest of your life—you were dropped. I am driven to tell you that this is not a self-inflicted wound. It's not your fault; you've been dropped, mishandled. Many sociopaths and psychopaths got their start in a life of crime because they too were dropped. Injured people injure people. I wonder who dropped the man who crippled me.

I lived my life through the process of a mishandled life, controlling women and indulging in sexual intercourse without the moral thought that what I was doing was wrong. It was the only way I could define myself as a man, the only way I could hide my pain. Only God knew what made me turn to women and not men, as I don't put one above the other, as we sometimes do religiously do. Sexual immorality is sexual immorality, sin is sin. Sigmund Freud, the father of psychology, described my behavior as psychosexual development disorder, and I recognize this as living through the process of a mishandled life.

We have all been mishandled by our caregiver, Adam, in the garden of Eden. We call it the Fall of Man. The entire human race was crippled by Adam's transgression, giving us inborn tendencies to commit certain acts of sin in our lives. The tendency may not always express itself sexually; it can also manifest socially, emotionally, or psychologically as intolerance, hatred, mistrust, lying, deceitfulness, and maliciousness, to name just a few. You were dropped. Now coping with it is living through the process. It was not self-inflicted; it was your caregiver, Adam. The reason that I say that Adam was our caregiver is that it was his responsibility to attend to the needs of humankind. God gave Adam dominion over the Earth, the right to set the example. When Adam disobeyed the direct orders of God and listened to the influence of another, he caused sin, transgression, to fall on all humankind. He set the example but not as God ordered. Thank God for the last Adam, the Lord Jesus Christ.

> Now unto him that is able to keep you from falling and to present you faultless before the presence of His glory with exceeding joy. To the only wise God our Savior, be glory and majesty, dominion and power, both now and ever amen. (Jude 1:24–25)

The only way out is to receive our new nature, which is holy, undefiled, blameless, in Christ Jesus, who loved us with His own life by giving His life on the cross, was resurrected on the third day, and is seated on the right hand of God. You don't have to stay crippled. God has new legs for you. Just as Mephibosheth is a picture of every person by the fall, Jesus Christ is a picture of every person by the cross.

I must confess and apologize to one of daughters, who was molested by her stepfather's brother when she was about five years old. She was dropped by her stepdad's brother, and she lived a promiscuous life as a result. The hardest thing for me to receive was when she told me that she was "born like that." I am so sorry that I tried to resist the truth and circumvent what I knew could be true. I thought that, once I gave my life to the Lord when she was four years old, my new life would destroy that generational seed of corruption. DNA is more than just a pool of genetic codes; it's also a vehicle by which sin is transferred from one generation to the next. I thought that giving my life to the Lord would have reversed the process of that mishandled life and destroyed that inherent condition, but I was wrong. I am so sorry she had to go through what she went through; I just didn't want to face the fact that, like me and like every other human, she was born with this truth, an incubator of sin within us waiting for our number to be called and for our issue to come forth.

Blessed be God the Father and Christ Jesus our Lord that God uses the process of life to bring us to the end of ourselves and save our souls. My prayer for everyone who reads this book is that the Lord brings you to the end of yourself and that the mistakes Adam made no longer control your life. Adam lost his life in the garden; don't let Adam lose your life now.

CHAPTER 4

Living Life out Of Bounds

And it came to pass afterward, that he loved the woman in the valley of Sorek, whose name was Delilah.

—Judges 16:4

Sorek was not a place easily found. In fact, the location is uncertain to this day. Approximately forty miles outside of Israelite territory, somehow Sampson wandered into this place and stumbled upon Delilah. Both the place and the woman were forbidden because Sampson was a Nazarite (Judges 16:2–5), one who was to be sanctified to Israelite territory, separated from strange women, never to touch a corpse, never to consume alcohol, and never to allow a razor to touch his head. Sampson was to be dedicated unto the

Lord for his entire life, and he had a unique gift from God, the strength of a thousand men as a sign of his consecration to God. Sampson's assignment from God was to protect Israel from its enemies, the Philistines. He was declared holy because of God's anointing and because he was of the chosen people of God.

However, Sampson had an inherent condition that he had received from Adam. He had a lust and a burning passion for Philistine women, who were out of bounds for him both by law and religiously. It was when he wandered outside his territory that he fastened his eyes upon Delilah, who most theologians believed was a cultic prostitute called a *qadesh*. It was a common practice of the Canaanites to employ women who were cultic prostitutes as a median between pagan gods and men. The Philistines, sea people from the Aegean Sea, were known as fierce warriors. Although the Canaanites hired them as mercenaries to fight their enemies, the Philistines eventually overthrew the Canaanites and took over their territory. Perhaps it was because they were fierce warriors with a pagan custom and culture that Delilah was committed to doing what she did.

Sampson was fascinated with Delilah's beauty and the sensuality—more than that, he was spell-bound, intoxicated, arrested, and ravished by her. However, inside her was the spirit of the Devil, which gave her her persuasive power. The lords of the Philistines, also captivated by Delilah, paid her to seduce Sampson so they could capture him. She was their perfect solution to their problem of how to bring about Sampson's demise.

Judges 16: 16 shows how, once Delilah coerced him with her words and mesmerized him with her beauty, Sampson laid his head on her lap and revealed where his power lay. Then the strongest man in the world was taken down and delivered in chains to a prison, all because of his weakness for the beauty of a woman. How did this happen? He was living life out of bounds. He went where he was not supposed to go and did what he was not supposed to do.

Sampson's fall was not sudden; it was subtle, slow, and quiet but certain. It was erosion at its best. When one falls hard, it never just happens. For instance, a person who is addicted to crack cocaine probably did not begin with crack, and a person who is a pedophile may have started with pornography. Sin never stops where it begins; there's always a progression that leads you out of bounds.

When you are living life out of bounds, it begins to eat at everything within you that defines who you are. It will destroy your morals and render your convictions ineffective, giving you an attraction, a fascination with everything that is outside your character. Spell-bound and intoxicated until the question of whether what you are doing is wrong is far removed, you no longer question whether something is right or wrong; it's just become a way of life.

I testified earlier about my life as a fornicator, but I was not always like that. I once was an innocent seventeen-year-old playing the drums at a church in my community. One evening after rehearsal, an older married woman approached me and asked whether I had heard of the song, "Secret Lovers." I replied that I did not. She responded, "Well, that's who we are." The next thing I knew, I was in her house, out of bounds, doing what I shouldn't have been doing. It was at that moment that the seed of fornication that was lying dormant within me came alive. By the time I was eighteen, I had already slept with several women who were much older than I was. I was no longer interested in church, and I began to lose my passion for playing the drums. I was living a life of high risk, chasing women from nightclub to nightclub and living life out of bounds. My life was taking a downward spiral, and I swiftly lost contact with who I was and my purpose in life. I had contracted a demon that used my body to do its will, and I was paying the price. My life was controlled by a spirit of fornication, and I had no thought for my life or the lives of others. I was living life out of bounds.

The strange thing about all of this promiscuity was that I did it all while I was saved, yet I was exposed to the threat of hell. However, even the threat of hell was not enough to stop me. It is possible to be saved and in a good position but have bad behavior. That's why it is not good to prejudge people because of their actions; they may be temporarily living out of bounds, and just because they are living out of bounds does not mean they are not saved.

> To all that be in Rome, beloved of God, called *to be* saints: grace to you and peace from God our father and the Lord Jesus Christ. (Romans 1:7 KJV)

Let's focus on the part of Romans 1:7 that says "called to be saints". The words "to be" are italicized, which means that they were inserted and not found in the original Greek manuscript. Therefore, the Scripture is spoken in past tense and not in future tense, so it should read, "to all that be in Rome, beloved of God, called saints." The same people that Paul called saint he describes by the end of the same chapter as being involved in all kinds of immoral behavior. This Scripture is not the doctrine of inclusion, nor is it a license to live in sin, but what it does say is that every believer in the Lord Jesus Christ is still a work in progress. I believe that we are perfect in Christ positionally but that conditionally we have issues under Christ. I believe, if we focus more on our position in Christ, that alone will change our condition under Christ. We need to teach the people of God more of what they are in Christ and focus less on what we are not under Christ.

> Not knowing that the goodness of God leadeth thee to repentance. (Romans 2:4 KJV)

When I met Rev. Frantz C. Dunn, III, who had just been installed as the pastor of Pilgrim Missionary Baptist Church in New Orleans, Louisiana, the Word of God and the gospel of the Lord Jesus Christ came alive for me. It was through his ministry that I learned not only that I was saved but how I was saved, and as a result my life and my behavior began to change.

Sampson's eyes were gouged out and he was thrown into a prison because he was out of bounds. Through his blindness he was able to see what was already before him and came to understand who he was in God and who God was in him. Isaiah said it was in the year that King Uziah died that he saw the Lord. Paul the apostle was on the Damascus road on his way to waste the church when God blinded his natural eyes only to open his spiritual eyes to reveal his son Christ Jesus to him. It was through my mess that God revealed Himself, not when I changed or made anything better. Jesus Christ came into the core of my heart and redirected my life. Praise be unto God. Now, as Paul said in Hebrews 12:2, I look unto Jesus, who is the author and finisher of my faith.

CHAPTER 5

Civil War

In 1863 America was experiencing one of the worse wars ever waged on American soil. It was when this great country fought against itself: the American Civil War. I believe that the greatest battle you will ever fight is the battle within *yourself*.

There are opposing natures in every person: the flesh and the spirit. The civil war between them is a fact of human existence.

> For the good that I would I do not: but the evil which I would not, that I do. Now if I do that I would not, it is no more I that do it, but sin that dwelleth in me. (Romans 7:19–20 KJV)

Or shall I say, "the Adam in me."

> [B]ut I see another law in my members warring against the law of my mind, and bringing me into captivity to the law of sin which is in my members. (Romans 7:23 KJV)

What is this if it is not civil war in the mind of a person because of the impulses of the body (the flesh) and memories of the pleasure of sin.

Two parts of your brain come into play as it relates to Civil War, the *substantia nigra* and the *cerebral cortex*. The neurotransmitter called dopamine is released from the *substantia nigra*, the part of your brain that causes you to feel both pain and pleasure at the same time, while the cerebral cortex is responsible for conscience and memory. Once your body figures out through the data of the cerebral cortex that it is rewarded with dopamine because of a certain behavior, it starts to crave that behavior in order to supply the brain with the dopamine. This is how addiction works and how withdrawal starts when it's deprived of the dopamine. Therefore, addictions are not just the result of ingesting alcohol or drugs, as one can experience the same effects of dopamine through addictions to sex, pornography, theft, lying, and other sins that are repetitive behaviors. We can sometimes be misled to think that it's the pleasure that produces the "high," when actually it is sometimes the pain, the civil war. That is how people sometimes choose to remain in abusive relationships; it's not the pleasure but the pain. That is also how you can become attracted to things, including people, that are not even attractive to you.

> For the flesh lusted against the spirit, and the spirit against the flesh: these are contrary the one to the other, so that you cannot do the things that you would. (Galatians 5:17 KJV)

Civil War!

In Romans 7:14–25 Paul uses the personal pronoun "I" twenty-seven times to let us know that the problem he was having was not with the *enemy* but with his *inner self*. The problem I experienced was not with the "me" you see but with the "me" that you don't see. Every individual wrestles with something within himself or herself and with his or her thoughts. The key to dealing with your thoughts is to conclude that *your thoughts are not always your person* (they are not who you are) nor is your person always your thoughts. Somehow Satan has entry into the spirit of your mind and thoughts such that he tries to entertain the mind with his thoughts as he did with Eve in the Garden in Genesis 2:1–7.

Your mind is where thoughts pop up, but your brain is where the thoughts originate.

Your mind is not your brain, and your brain is not your mind. Your brain is like a CPU, a central processing unit: it's a database of processed information, both good and evil. Your mind is your spirit, personality, choice, and spiritual consciousness. The Devil uses information recorded in your brain to influence your mind/spirit, which produces the struggle, the civil war. As 2 Corinthians 10:3 (KJV) says, "For though we walk in the flesh, we do not war after the flesh."

The Devil uses thoughts like digital information and develops them into pictures in your mind/spirit through positioning. Positioning puts a thought in your mind and develops a certain emotional response so images pop into your spirit and wage war against your conscience, leaving you prey to your thoughts. If you are not watchful, the Devil's thoughts can sound just like you, but they are not. He just mimics your sound.

> For the weapons of our warfare are not carnal but mighty through God to the pulling down of strongholds. Casting down imaginations and every high thing that exalteth itself against knowledge of God, and bringing into captivity every thought to obedience of Christ. (2 Corinthians 10:4–5 KJV)

Dealing with Uninformed Conversations

You don't have to fall victim to your thoughts. Christ Jesus has given you power over your thoughts. The Devil knows your struggles with the spiritual war inside of you and appeals to that injured, confused, troubled part of your being. The Devil is at war with the flesh to control your thoughts and make you captive to do its will instead of God's.

The dictionary defines "uninformed" as not having or showing awareness or understanding of the facts, so the conversation you have with the Devil is uninformed conversation. There is no announcement or warning for when and where the Devil comes, and it does not matter to him where you are geographically, as some of the worst thoughts came to mind in the most inopportune places, like church fellowship or while you are with your family. Be honest: you did not set out to see such images or think such thoughts, and they don't represent who are you are as a person. That is why the conversation is uninformed; it happens without warning.

> And I knew such a man (whether in the body, or out of the body) I cannot tell: God knoweth. How that he was caught up into paradise and heard unspeakable words, which is not lawful for a man to utter. Lest I should be exalted

above measure through the abundance of the revelation, there was given me a thorn in the flesh, the messenger of Satan to buffet me. (2 Corinthians 12:3, 4, 7 KJV)

The Greek word for messenger is *angelo*, which means to bring tidings or information. In Matthew chapter 4 and Luke chapter 4, Jesus Christ was tempted by the Devil. Jesus started in the wilderness but was in Jerusalem in a moment of time. How did He get there so fast? The Devil took Him through His thoughts. In each of these cases, the Devil didn't announce that he was coming. He did not ask for the right of entry. The conversation was uninformed. Paul prayed to God and the Lord Jesus Christ used the Word of God to defeat the Devil.

They switched the channel.

Finally brethren, whatsoever things are true, whatsoever things are honest, whatsoever things are just, whatsoever things are pure, whatsoever things are lovely, whatsoever things are of good report; if there be any virtue, and if there be any praise, think on these things. (Phillipians 4:8 KJV)

What is Paul suggesting when he says "think on these things"? When it relates to civil war in the mind/spirit, we have to use our mind/spirit like we use a remote control on a television: we switch the channel when we don't like what we see. When your thoughts interrupt you, you interrupt your thoughts. Sometimes my wife asks if I'm saying something, and I say, "I'm just thinking out loud." What I am doing in thinking aloud is saying to my mind/spirit, "No, I rebuke that" or "I am not receiving that." Sometimes I am just quoting a Scripture. This is how you win the civil war: cast it down "[a]nd be renewed in the spirit of your mind …. Neither give place to the devil" (Ephesians 4:23, 27).

CHAPTER 6

The Practical Dilemma

The word *practical* comes from the Greek word *praktikos*, meaning fit for action. A dilemma is a situation that is usually equally unfavorable; either way you lose something.

> For the good that I would I do not: but the evil which I would not, that I do. Now if I do that I would not, it is no more I that do it but sin that dwelleth in me. I find then a law that when I would do good evil is present with me. (Romans 7:19–21 KJV)

Living life can sometimes be a practical dilemma when the urge to do what is wrong is as strong as the desire to do what is right. When I do wrong, my spirit loses, and when

I do right, my flesh loses. One way or the other, I lose. We must understand that losing has a purpose, as through losing one can achieve success, freedom, and deliverance. Losing is okay when it helps you discover the true results of success: freedom and happiness. When you learn what not to do, you have also discovered what to do. Therefore, losing becomes a catalyst by which success, freedom, and happiness are revealed.

The practical dilemma can be difficult when deciding which side of our nature should take the loss for the greater good, as we don't like losing even if we know that we are losing for a good reason. As a result, we sometimes play the middle ground, which never works out.

Addictive behavior is intensified, and withdrawal symptoms occur because your conscious self knows that this is a practical dilemma: I don't want to lose, but if I walk away, I lose, and if I commit, I lose. Here is where the struggle begins.

For me, sex was no longer a pleasure; it was an addictive behavior. If I didn't do it, I experienced symptoms of withdrawal, perspiring and trembling uncontrollably just like a person addicted to heroin does. My dilemma kicked in. If I pursue sex, I lose because I know it's not right. And, if I don't, I lose because my bones will ache because I'm not feeding my habit.

> Whosoever seeks to save his life shall lose it; and whosoever shall lose his life shall preserve it. (Luke 17:33 KJV)

> For me to live is Christ; and to die is gain. (Phillipians 1:21 KJV)

Both of these Scriptures present a practical dilemma for the believer. It sounds like a paradox, but in dying you live, and in losing you gain. Here's where the practical dilemma hurts, as self-preservation doesn't want the flesh to suffer. Even Satan suggested to God, "Skin for skin, yea, all that a man hath will he give for his life" (Job 2:4 KJV).

Our concept of crucifixion has been contaminated and fabricated by its outcome, which is death, Crucifixion is a slow, suffering death. In some cases, people would hang on crosses for days before dying. Practical dilemmas are designed to produce suffering so the power of God may be manifested in our habits, addictions, and the issues from which we've been asking God to deliver us. God manifests Himself by allowing practical dilemmas and showing Himself greater *in* it than it is, while causing you to die *to* it.

Let me give you an example of dying to something. Say you went to a cemetery and found the grave of a former alcoholic, and you placed a bottle of vodka, wine, or beer on top of the grave. If you came back the same time the next day, you would discover that the person in the grave had not touched it because that person is dead and dead to it. The practical dilemma reveals the need for us to die more to self.

> And he said unto me, My grace is sufficient for thee: for my strength is made perfect in weakness. (2 Corinthians 12:9 KJV)

Why did God leave the thorn in Paul's flesh instead of removing it as Paul requested? What God is doing through practical dilemmas is bringing us to the end of Adam, the end of self.

> For whom he did foreknow, he also did predestinate *to be* conformed to the image of his Son. (Romans 8:29 KJV)

As human beings, we never evolved from anything, but as believers, we are constantly evolving into the image of Christ.

CHAPTER 7

Demonic Attendance

> Peter therefore was kept in prison; but prayer was made without ceasing of the church unto God for him. And when Herod would have brought him forth, the same night Peter was sleeping between two soldiers, bound with two chains and keepers before the door kept the prison.
>
> —Acts 12:5–6

Peter is in prison, sleeping between two soldiers and keepers at the door. Peter is bound in chains, and the prison doors have been locked. Why is there a need for so much protection to keep one man in bondage? Peter is not a normal inmate; he's a man of God with the anointing of God and on a mission for God. The soldiers are symbolic of demonic behavior. If you are in bondage, Satan has assigned his demons to see to it that you stay in bondage until he's ready to deliver you up for death.

I call this *demonic attendance*. Adam's actions subjected every person to it. Some demonic attendance is generational, some is territorial, and some is strategically assigned to people and places. Daniel 10: 13 stipulates that the prince of Persia, who is a demon, kept the angel of God from bringing Daniel word. Michael, the warring angel, had to defeat the demon of Persia before the angel, Gabriel, could respond to Daniel's request.

The apostle Paul talks about demonic attendance in Ephesians 6:12–13, where he describes how demons are assigned to areas in a series of powers. Demons are in ranks like our military forces (generals, majors, lieutenants, corporals, and privates), with Satan himself as commander and chief. The word *argus*, from the Greek word *argos*, which refers to cities, towns, or principalities, represents a series of powers. These are fallen angels who left their first estate and were thrown out of heaven with Satan (2 Peter 2:4).

Let me share with you how my life evolved to a level of demonic engagement. When I was five years old I heard voices from the unseen world. I was afraid of the dark because every night I was tortured by a demonic presence. I wasn't raised in a Christian home, nor did I have a religious background, so I didn't know what to do. To make matters worse, my dad thought that I was just scared of the dark. He once made a dummy, put a speaker behind it, called my name through the speaker, and watched me scream in terror and tear my room apart. He thought it was funny. No one knew that my life had been traumatized and that I was captive in a spiritual and psychological prison cell that no one could see but me. The voices I heard increased until I felt a fearful, evil presence watching me all the time.

When I was eighteen years old, I moved into my own apartment. Whenever I woke in the night, I was afraid to open my eyes because I felt an evil presence watching me. One night in particular, I woke up in the middle of the night and saw what appeared to be a witch's hand coming through my window to get me. This experience drove me farther into a life of fornication; I was so scared that I had to bring a woman home every night so I wouldn't have to be alone. The days were fine, but nights were a nightmare that ended only when the sun came up. This continued until I was twenty-two years old.

One night at about 3:00 am, I was alone. I had symptoms of withdrawal, with drops of sweat falling from my face and uncontrollable trembling. Finally, the demon spoke out forcibly within the spirit of my mind and said, "Get the knife and kill yourself. You don't need to live like this anymore." Now my fear, my conscience, and my withdrawals met together for the first time. At that moment I realized that demons were not the only ones watching and assigned to me, as an angelic presence spoke to me and said, "Pray." I cried out desperately that night and said to God, "If you remove this spirit from me, I will give you my life completely." I don't remember falling asleep that night—I think I just passed out—but at daybreak, my heart was different than it had been the day before. Something had happened to me: God changed my heart, and my desires were no longer the same.

A few years ago I had a vision in which a tall man—about nine feet tall—was running after me. He was so wide and tall that I was afraid to look at him. He chased me down a long, wooded street, where there was no house in sight, but ahead of me there was a wide canal filled with water. As I ran, I thought that there was no way that this big man could jump over this canal, so if I jumped over it, I'd be free. I ran desperately and lunged across the canal, but before I landed on the other side, he was already there. Out of fear, I punched him, and he looked at me and smiled. I punched him again, and he smiled again, looking at me with an expression of great joy and concern. I was captivated and arrested, and when I came out of the vision, I realized that he was an angel assigned to me by God to keep me in His ways. I recognized that I had been running and fighting the very thing that God had sent to help me.

> For He gives His angels charge over thee to keep thee in all thy ways. (Psalm 90:11 KJV)

In my twenty-plus years of ministry, people have testified that demons even crawled into bed with them and tried to force them to have sex while they were asleep. My response was to ask them to tell me about the hidden sin, that stronghold that was on their lives. You see, demons have to have a door to work through, a stronghold somewhere where you are in bondage to the Devil. I encouraged them to confess their hidden issues because confession exposes the enemy and breaks the stronghold so true deliverance can take place.

> Or else, how can one enter into a strongman's house, and spoil his goods, except he first bind the strongman? Then he shall spoil his house. (Matthew 12:29 KJV)

The Devil uses various avenues as a means of entry into your psychological, social, and emotional being to manipulate, contaminate, and control your everyday life. He uses sexual immorality, such as fornication, sexual promiscuity, and pornography. He uses socialization and entertainment by way of drugs, alcohol, gambling, television, radio, and music as a means to bind you and spoil your spiritual house.

One of the most notorious serial killers, Ted Bundy, said in an interview that it was his addiction to pornography that began when he was a child that tore down his respect for human life and caused him to murder. Pornography was the door the Devil used to bind Ted Bundy, but you never know how far a demon that's been attending to you will take you. Confession breaks the stronghold that's on your life. Speak with someone who is connected to God who can pray with you through the Word of God.

I was freed that night that I cried out to God. That was the night the Lord brought me to the end of myself. What I have learned over the years since was that my actions were controlled by an evil spirit that had been lurking around my family for generations on both my mother's and my father's sides. *I was born like this.* These were tools the Devil used to try to destroy me and my ministry, but blessed be God our Father and the Lord Jesus Christ, who has always caused us to triumph.

More than sixteen years ago, when God commissioned me to start the ministry, Faith Praise and Deliverance Temple, I wrestled with four territorial demons in that community: incest, witchcraft (voodoo), murder, and the spirit of religious tradition. These spirits were all opposing demons to the ministry that God had established. It took several years before God revealed to me the spirits I was fighting against and how I was to overcome them. They were the demonic attendants that had been there for decades, assigned to keep this community in spiritual bondage. The first wave of attack from those spirits was character assassination, then mental fatigue, and then spiritual burnout.

The Devil started spiritual brush fires within the ministry to distract me from the direction that God had assigned me to go. I found myself going in circles to put out the brush fires, distracting me from the bigger issues that needed my attention. I call this demonic diversion, when smaller issues keep popping up to capture your attention in efforts to distract you from the bigger issues that need you. I started noticing a wicked spirit trying to usurp authority over those I assigned as leaders in our fellowship. I saw the spirit of jealousy, envy, and manipulation. Then I recognized that all these spirits were the symptoms of the spirit of Jezebel, the mother of all rebellion, witchcraft, deceit, and manipulation. Bless the Lord for apostle Jonas Clark, who through his books and conferences, helped me to identify that spirit and remove it from our church fellowship.

Just when I thought that the fight couldn't get worse, the Enemy attacked several key members of our fellowship with deadly sicknesses and diseases, including tumors in the brain, strokes, heart attacks, sclerosis of the liver, pancreatic cancer, and prostate cancer, but Praise be to God, all of them were divinely healed!

Even though we experienced these attacks on the ministry, we can testify to many victories. Our local bars have been closed. The drug dealers no longer control our corners. Many of the drug addicts are no longer using and have been set free. Countless young couples who were living together outside of wedlock are now married. Juvenile violence and teen pregnancy has significantly decreased. What's more, after thirty years, we were able to bring a carnival festival back into our community that was both drug- and alcohol-free and that promoted family and community unity. According to our local police, not one altercation or incident took place during the festivities. We also hosted a Community Unity Day to bring everyone together.

I'd like to share some of the strategies that God instructed us to use that brought about this significant change in our community. We held a seven-day prayer revival and a twenty-four-hour prayer vigil. During the prayer vigil, we prayed every hour on the hour. God also instructed us to go into the community and divide up into four groups, with each group assigned to a specific street corner in the community to pray. The corners God sent us to were the very spots where distribution of drugs and gambling took place. After one of our neighborhood prayer watches, the police came the next day and arrested all of the drug dealers. We held worship services outside in various places in the community instead of holding services at our church. We set specific periods for our church fellowship to fast and pray. Finally, we removed religious traditions that had their roots or origin in pagan customs: we do not operate by calendar, nor do we hold calendared events such as pastors' anniversaries. Because we've reformed our worship, we are directed by the Holy Spirit and are, therefore, sensitized to the spirit of God and move by God's assignment.

In the book of Kings, Josiah was a great king because of his reformation, and Ezra was a great priest because of his reformation. I am not suggesting that our community is perfect, but we are making great strides in the spirit.

> For though we walk in the flesh, we do not war after the flesh. For the weapons of our warfare are not carnal but mighty through God to the pulling down of strong holds. (2 Corinthians 10:3–4 KJV)

It was through prayer that we received instructions from God to act upon. When a church becomes controlled and programmed by calendared events, it misses out on valuable instructions from God that bring about a significant movement in the community. A demonic presence has been assigned to every community, so it is essential that the church become visible in the community and not withdrawn behind its walls. We must engage, not retreat, in the face of conflict, for God has called us to conflict, not recess; to vocation, not vacation.

CHAPTER 8

Repeat Offender

> And when the devil had ended all temptation, he departed from him for a season.
>
> —Luke 4:13(KJV)

The wilderness experience is one of several encounters Jesus had with Satan. When Jesus was born in the flesh, he was born into an atmosphere of a demonic presence headed by Satan, the offender. A repeat offender is a person who's already been convicted for a crime and whose behavior has not changed.

Since the beginning of time, Satan's *modus operandi* or his M.O., way of doing things has not changed, so he is a repeat offender. In many ways Satan has influenced us to become repeat offenders as well. Consider what Jesus said in John

10:10: "The thief cometh not, but for to steal, and to kill, and to destroy." The thief comes only if his intent is to steal, kill, and destroy—to steal your joy, kill your dreams, and destroy your life. Doesn't that sound like a familiar pattern?

This is why Scripture says that God has informed us about the Devil's devices, as God wants us to recognize the Devil's approach and arm ourselves. For eighteen years I have been consecrated to the Lord and my wife. I have not touched, kissed, or communicated with another woman in a way unbecoming a man of God. Amen, to God be the glory. Even so, I have not had two days free of the repeat offender's harassment. He is always lurking nearby to see if I will maintain my integrity.

You see, Satan knows where you've been and where you came from. He does not sit back and applaud you for getting out of bondage; his mind set is to pull you back in. I remember one night when I was sleeping at the altar at the church building, which I often do to consecrate before God. Sleeping in the church holds no benefits of holiness; I just like spending time with God alone, praying and meditating on the Word. That night I dreamed I was having indecent relations with two women of a different ethnic decent. I experienced a realistic, ungodly dream while sleeping at the altar spending time with God. When I awoke out of my sleep, I ran out of the church and said I'd never sleep in the church again. How could this happen to me? I felt alone, filthy, and ashamed. Then the Lord spoke persuasively in my spirit and said, "Hold your head up. That was not you! I allowed Satan to do that to you so you would know what it would feel like if you did do that." Immediately my joy was restored, and I felt clean again.

About a month after that, the two women I had dreamed joined the church, although I recognized only one of them. One afternoon I was studying alone in my office, and one of the women came into my office, lay down on the chaise lounge, and opened her legs. I felt that demon spirit leap onto me, but I ran out of the office, went next door to my house, and got my son to ask one of the sisters to come to the church and get her out. She later called and apologized and said she felt a need that she just had to have me. I explained to her that I loved the Lord, I love my wife, and I loved the ministry. I explained to her that the Devil wants my anointing and I am not giving it up, it doesn't come cheap.

What I should have told her as well, as I later recognized, was that it was not her, it was the repeat offender. What would have happened if God had not forewarned me by allowing Satan to send me that dream? God allowed Satan to attack me in three ways that day: the young woman was beautiful, we were alone, and my flesh wanted what it wanted. The Devil knows what you like and where you have been, so you can look for Satan to try you with what is already within you. He does not use foreign materials.

> But every man is tempted, when he is drawn away of his own lust and enticed. Then when lust hath conceived, it bringeth forth sin: and sin, when it is finished, bringeth forth death. (James 1: 14–15)

Satan, the repeat offender, does not use foreign materials; he uses what is already there. A thief does not break in because of what is without but what is within. Satan's job is pulling out what is within.

Several years ago I preached at the church in New Orleans where I first accepted my calling into the ministry. I'd been gone for more than twelve years. After my sermon and the worship service were over, I was walking out when a young woman who had been at that church all of her life stopped me and said, "You don't have to call me after. You don't have to see me again. Just sleep with me one time."

I responded, "I am sorry, but I don't do that."

She said, "I didn't mean it; I just wanted to see if you were for real."

That was the repeat offender. He does not care where you are or what you may have just done for God; he knows where you've been.

In 2 Corinthians 12:1–9 the apostle Paul was in the third heaven in paradise before God, when the repeat offender came in, and Revelation 12:11, "And they overcame him by the blood of the Lamb and by the word of their testimony." I find that, the more I share my testimony, the stronger I become. It's as if God establishes a law in me every time I tell it, to God be the Glory. The woman with the issue of blood who was made whole was healed but didn't become whole until she said for what cause she touched Him: *she testified.*

CHAPTER 9

Attempt to Abort the Next Great Thing

Then Herod, when he saw that he was mocked of the wise men, was exceedingly wroth, and sent forth, and slew all the children that were born in Bethlehem.

—Matthew 2:16 (KJV)

And he said when you do the office of a midwife to the Hebrew women, and see them upon the stools; if it be a son, then ye shall kill him.

—Exodus 1:16 (KJV)

These two Scriptures have a thematic connection, where one is a type and the other an anti-type. Finding a thematic connection is to find the pattern and know the truth. It is a formula that we use when cross-referencing Scripture to give correct context to its meaning. The type is a picture of Christ, the anti-type is Christ himself. Each Scripture shows an attempt to murder or abort the birth of "the next great thing," which was the deliverer of the nation of Israel. Jesus Christ and Moses, two of the greatest deliverers who ever lived, had this connection.

In the context of the Scriptures, this was abortion at its fullest. Hundreds of thousands—perhaps millions—of babies' lives were aborted trying to stop the next great thing. Herod and Pharaoh, symbolic of the Devil, were enraged and trying to stop what was predestined of God to save generations of people and affect the world for all eternity.

The word *abort* comes from a Latin word *aboriri*, which means miscarry, pass, disappear, or be lost. The Latin prefix *ab* means away from or off mark, while *oriri* means to be born or rise. When you put the words together, you have "off mark to be born or rise" *Aboriri* acknowledges that something is or was there and that something was purposely lost through no fault of its own. Some say that abortion is the termination of a pregnancy, but it is the termination of life. Whether it is before the wound or after the wound, it is the termination of life.

Moses, Mother Teresa, Dr. Martin Luther King, Jr., Abraham Lincoln, the Wright brothers, Nelson Mandela, and Mahatma Gandhi are all people who probably considered themselves normal prior to their fame, but they had exceptional expectation for their lives, and they were world-changers. What precious personalities and contributors to humanity we would have lost if they had been "born away or off the mark"? My mother, Gloria Blue Lee, is in my opinion the greatest woman who ever lived. She conceived me when she was fourteen and gave birth to me at fifteen. I wonder if she ever considered abortion. She was only fourteen, her mother had died when she was only a year old, and her dad had emotionally scarred her, so she had an excuse if ever there was one. What about Mary, the mother of the Lord Jesus Christ, or the mothers of all the other world-changers I've mentioned? What would society be like today if they were "born away or off the mark"?

I help to support my mother—she lives in my guest house—and I hope to build or buy her a house someday. I would die a thousand deaths before I would turn my back on my mother. What blessings she would have lost had she aborted me. What blessings the world would have lost had Herod been successful in preventing Christ from being born.

There is another kind of abortion that affects humanity every day that sometimes goes undetected: spiritual abortion. Through spiritual abortion Satan is trying to stop the next great thing.

How many visions, dreams and aspirations have been considered off the mark to be born or rise because of some tragic moment that happened in life? The world's next great thing stopped because the person assigned to it had been mishandled or dropped. Unlike physical abortions, spiritual abortions can be reversed.

In 1997 my dad, Martin Luther Lee, Sr., in my view one of the greatest men who ever lived said to me one day, "Otis, you are the minister in the family. You ought to start Bible class because the family is falling apart." I didn't grow up in a religious home, but by then I had been in ministry for more than six years and was an associate minister at Hill of Zion Baptist Church under the leadership of Rev. Alan K. Creecy, Sr. We started having family Bible Study with about eight people in my parents' living room on Friday nights. After a month or two, attendance grew beyond my family, and someone asked, "When will we start the church?"

I responded, "Start a church? No, I have helped others start churches before—too much work and too many sacrifices. Besides all this, to my knowledge there was neither land to buy nor any buildings available to renovate to start a church." What's more, many of the people who were attending the Bible study were "un-churched" (people who had no commitment to church fellowship) street people, prostitutes, and fornicators.

Then the Lord spoke through one of those who attended, Bro. Ronnie Smith, who said, "Do the work of the church; be the church and God will provide you a building."

My wife and I incorporated the fellowship under the name of Faith, Praise and Deliverance Temple and started having church services in the front yard of my parents' home. One day, thirty minutes into the service, some people in the community called the police complaining of disturbance of the peace. It was an attempt to stop the next great thing, to render us off the mark to be born or rise.

We later moved to an old, run-down hall that the community was no longer using and made the necessary repairs to it. Lo and behold, the ministry started growing at a surprising rate, but then some of the community leaders got together and told us that the community did not need another church. People in the community had been murdered, some were on crack and breaking into houses, women were on the streets selling their bodies to supply their habits, and men were on the corners gambling and pushing drugs, refusing to get out of the way of anyone who drove down the streets, daring them to hit them. We didn't need another church in this community?

The community leaders applied pressure on the parish official of the parks and recreation department, and with tears in his eyes he was forced to put us out. It was an attempt to stop the next great thing.

We moved to a nearby park, and again they called the police, but we continued to have services in that park for about a month and a half. During that time we were able to purchase some property in the community in an area zoned as wetlands and started developing it. The pastor of the New Jerusalem Baptist Church, Rev. Henry LeBoyd, Jr., offered to share his church sanctuary with us to hold our worship services and graciously allowed us to worship there for two and a half years. As our ministry continued to grow, I received a tip that an old building was available on the west bank of the Mississippi River in Taft, Louisiana, where the New Union Baptist Church had once worshiped. The building had been closed down for many years and was in desperate need of repairs, so the property caretaker allowed us to rent it for $300 per month if we would repair the building. After two and a half years there, the Lord led me to talk to the President of St. Charles Parish, Albert Laque, about the building where we had held services eight years earlier. The building was rarely used, was falling apart, and had become an eyesore in the community. Mr. Laque agreed to let us lease the building and do the necessary repairs. The day after my meeting with Mr. Laque, a representative from a community association presented Mr. Laque with a petition from 250 citizens in the community, stating that the building was beyond repair, that it had outlived its purpose, and that it should be torn down. This was another attempt to abort the next great thing.

Parish President Laque told the representative that he'd met with me the day before and had agreed to lease me the building. He suggested that the community representative contact me in order to come to some type of agreement. Even with the 250 signatures, Mr. Laque was not willing to negate the agreement made with me. This experience showed me how important it is to move when God says move; had I waited one more day, I would have been too late.

The community representative came to my home and shared with me what they wanted to do, and I shared with him what the Lord wanted me to do. Angry, he said, "We are going to tear this building down! We are going to fight you!"

I replied, "Not me, God! It is His work that I am doing, not my own."

The representative then asked me to come to the community meeting, where the panel tried to persuade me to abort what God wanted me to do. Of course, I was not moved, so no agreement was made. Later that week, the group came up with the idea that I could have the building if I moved it somewhere else. The expectation was that, because it was so old, it would crumble as it was being moved to the new location. Little did they know that that old building was made of Cyprus wood, one of the most expensive and durable natural substances. Such a building could stand for another century. It is important that you do not receive the negative words and actions of others as they relate to your life.

In biblical times, names identified a person's purpose and were essential to their lives.

> Now among these were of the children of Judah, Daniel, Hananiah, Mishael, and Azariah. (Daniel 1:6 KJV)

These men were Jewish captives in Babylon, where Hebrew names represented a particular need God had for the people of God. Many of their names had the suffix of "iah"–pronounced "yah"—which the holy name of God first mentioned in Scripture to Moses in Exodus 6:3. Consider the meanings of their names and how the Babylonians changed them. In Hebrew, Daniel means "God is my Judge," but it was changed to a Babylonian name, Belteshazzar, meaning "Prince of Bel (Baal)." Hananiah means "Jah, who is gracious," but it was changed to Shadrach, meaning "command of the moon god." Azariah means "Jah has helped," but it was changed to Meshach, which means "who is what Aku." Mishael means "who is like God," but it was changed to Abednego, which means "servant of Nebo/Nabu."

The changed names all refer to pagan/idol gods. When the Enemy changes your name, it is because he wants to take you "off the mark." The community association called me crazy when I wanted to keep that building—the work of the Devil in attempting to get me off the mark to rise. Why do you suppose the Babylonians changed the three Hebrew boy's names? Changing their names was an attempt to abort the next great thing, and the Babylonians would have been successful in their attempt if the Hebrew boys had not known who they were and the significance of their names. It does not matter what the Enemy calls you; what does matter is what *you* call you. The Enemy was trying to render them "off mark to rise." They did not rise in Judah, but they rose mightily in Babylon, where God had intended.

> Therefore I make a decree, that every people, nation and language, which speak anything amiss against the God of Shadrach, Meshach and Abednego shall be cut in pieces, and their houses shall be made a dunghill because there is no other God that can deliver after this sort. Then the King promoted Shadrach, Meshach and Abednego in the province of Babylon.
> (Daniel 3:29–30 KJV)

The three Hebrew boys were slaves/captives, but there were the next great thing in Babylon. Life does not start with a fetus; it starts with the purpose of God.

> My substance was not hid from thee, when I was made in secret, and curiously wrought in the lowest parts of the earth. Thine eyes did see my substance yet being unperfect. (Psalm 139:15–16 KJV)

> Before I formed thee in the belly I knew thee; and before thou camest forth out of the wound I sanctified thee, and ordained thee a prophet unto the nations. (Jeremiah 1:5 KJV)

Consider the meaning of "Jeremiah": Yah, meaning "God uplifts." Don't let the enemy change your name. My name, Otis, means "keen of hearing." Thank God that I listen to His voice.

Now let me tell you what happened with our fellowship and the building. The association again met with President Laque, and he consented to their suggestion that the building be given to me if I moved it. The paperwork was drawn up, but we were faced with another dilemma since we didn't have the money to move it. My wife and I decided that we would take out a mortgage on our home in order to move the building and give it back to God and the people of my town of New Sarpy. Praises be to God, after nine years of wandering, God provided the very building from which they had evicted us eight years earlier.

The building was approximately one hundred years old. It was once a hall in the city of Norco, Louisiana, in a community called Belltown, which Shell Chemical Refinery bought out in 1969 and relocated to the Diamond Plantation subdivision. Many of the residents of Belltown and Diamond Plantation were descendants of slaves, and many Gospel greats had sung in that building, including Mahalia Jackson. Many weddings, benefit suppers, receptions, and parties had been held in that hall. What a blessing that it had been bestowed upon me to preserve a hundred years of history in two communities in which I grew up. To God be the Glory!

Regardless of the Enemy's attempts, I never strayed from my mission. I moved the worship service from Taft, Louisiana, to my house in New Sarpy because we wanted to preserve every dollar to repair the building. We had services there for a year while I worked with my own hands to repair the building along with others who supported the vision of this ministry. After that year, we were finished, and it is now one of the prettiest buildings in all of St. Charles Parish. As for New Sarpy, after sixteen years of ministry, our children can walk the streets without threat or harm. Our barrooms are closed, many of those addicted to drugs are delivered, and the drug dealers have either relocated or gone out of business. After nearly seventeen years of prison ministry, over a hundred thousand lives are different. The homeless have been sheltered, the hungry have been fed, homes have been spared from foreclosure, and financial assistance for utilities has been provided, and all with no government subsidies or outside contributions—all through God and the members of our fellowship.

> What shall we then say to these things? If God be for us, who can be against us? (Romans 8:31 KJV)

I believe that God will raise up a deliverer in every home, in every community, that both destined and destiny will meet if the home, the community, the people do not abort it. Everything about you—past, present and future—God knows and God has purposed.

I once preached a sermon called "Purposed," whose three points of focus were orchestrated, allowed, and tolerated. One way or another, God is somewhere in or behind everything that has happened in your purposed life. God was either in everything that happened to me, bringing me through it, or behind it, pushing me to it. God does not work haphazardly in our lives. Either He has control over everything or He doesn't; we cannot have it both ways.

I'd like to pose a question to you as you read this book: Are you the next great thing? If you don't think you are, remember this: God created you with a purpose. Therefore, I charge you: Don't allow yourself to be off the mark to be born or rise. Be the next great thing.

> In Rama was there a voice heard, lamentation, and weeping, and great mourning, Rachel weeping for her children, and would not be comforted, because they are not. (Matthew 2:18 KJV)

CHAPTER 10

The Aftermath

An aftermath is a consequence, especially that of a disaster or a misfortune.

> Be not deceived; God is not mocked; for whatsoever a man soweth, that shall he also reap. (Galatians 6:7 KJV)

The context of this Scripture is giving, but there is a principle we must glean from it, the Law of Reciprocity, the idea that what you give is what's given back to you, and what you sow is what you reap.

> While the earth remaineth, seed time and harvest, and cold and heat, summer and

winter, day and night shall not cease. (Genesis 8:22 KJV)

This Scripture has two components: what you plant is what you harvest and what goes around comes around. My former pastor, Frantz C. Dunn, III, used to tell me, "Whatever goes across the horse's back buckles up under his belly." I shared earlier about my molestation and identity crisis and how I indulged in a life of fornication and manipulating women to conceal pain, shame, fear, and inferiority. What I have not mentioned is the multiple children with multiple women I have as a result of my promiscuous life—that is, the aftermath or consequence. By age eighteen, I had already fathered two children with two women, four months apart. My mother came into my room at about two one morning, when I had just come in from the streets. She said to me, "You made them, and I'm going to see to it that you take care of them." She put one child in one of my arms and the other in the other arm. My mother would not make excuses for my behavior, and she was not about to see her grandchildren go without, so when I did not get these children from their mothers, she did, and she made me become a man and take care of my responsibilities. I lost a lot of youthful freedom because I ignorantly chose to enter into adulthood sooner than I was able to consider the consequences of my actions—the aftermath.

I hid the life that I was living from my children because I didn't want them to know what I had chosen. By the time I was twenty-two, I had three children to support. I created a maze for myself that I thought I would never find my way out of. I worked during the day and went to school at night, trying to better myself, and when Friday came, I had only $98.00 left after child support deductions. The spirit of hopelessness and depression set in. The nice apartment was gone, the fine clothing was wearing thin, and I had to give up my car. There was no longer enough money to support the wayward life I once lived. I had fornicated my way into bondage. What the Devil did not show me as he lured me deeper was that my careless actions would put me in an economic and emotional prison from which I thought I could never escape.

 I had taken a job at a florist, A Maison de Fleur, whose owner was Betty Portera. She taught me how to design flowers and manage her business. She introduced me to prominent people in St. Charles Parish and made them aware of both my loyalty and devotion in running her business. She saw the good in me and demonstrated her trust in me by giving me access to her bank accounts and credit cards. Once she even gave me $10,000 in cash to hold for two weeks! Ms. Portera later told me that she'd tested me many times and seen that I never took a dime. In one aspect of my life I was a person with multiple problems, hiding in the shadows of my past, but I was also a person who demonstrated trust, loyalty, and devotion. There was something in me worth harvesting, the "me" God intended me to be. There's some good in everything and in everyone, and we must be patient and disciplined enough to search it out.

In the early 1990s, I had to deliver a flower arrangement to East Jefferson Hospital in Metairie, Louisiana. While on my way there, I passed the car of one of my former classmates, who had just been in a terrible train wreck that had taken the lives of some of his relatives, although he escaped with minimal injuries. I thought, if I had had that experience so recently, there is no way that I'd be driving. At that moment, an authoritative voice spoke within me, saying, "Go talk to him. Tell him to stop what he's doing or he's going to get killed."

I responded within myself, "No, he knows me, he knows what I do." He knows the lifestyle that I'd once lived. The voice spoke again, more aggressively: "If you don't, his blood will be on your hands, and something bad will happen to you."

Again I responded, "I can't do it." I felt inadequate because my life was not perfect either.

It was the close of the day at the florist, but by the time I returned to the shop, there was a flower arrangement waiting to be delivered to that young man's home for his mother. I don't know who put the arrangement together, but it was there, waiting, so I had no choice; if I wanted to keep my job I had to make the delivery. I thought, I would take my own car since I'd be passing by his house on my way home anyway. I'd park my car in the middle of street, give his mother the arrangement, and leave.

When I got there, his mother answered the door. She had such a godly smile and personality that I was instantly arrested by her presence, and though I hadn't planned to, I asked if her son were home, as I had to speak to him. I ran back to pull my car off the road, and when I returned, she pointed me toward her living room and went to get him. I can see him walking down the hallway, as if it were yesterday.

He sat down next to me, and I said, "I don't know why God chose me to talk to you, but there is something in your life that God wants you to stop doing."

He responded, "I know, I just have to trust in God."

I left the house and felt a sense of relief because I would no longer hear that voice speaking to me. I went back to my partially promiscuous life, and about a month later I learned that he had been killed. That same day, that authoritative voice of God came to me, even more powerful than before, and said, "Quit running around after women and preach my gospel, or you will die of AIDS." I was so scared that I was trembling. I called my pastor and told him that God had called me to preach.

My pastor knew the problems I'd been having and replied, "Don't tell anyone else that. I think you are making a mistake." Later he called me and asked whether I was "sure about this preaching thing."

I responded, "Rev, I've got to preach!"

He paused a moment and then said, "I know. It was when you said 'I've got to.'"

I shared with my girlfriend that I had to get married because God had called me to preach, but she didn't believe me, nor did she believe that change had really taken place in my life, so we did not marry. I don't blame her for not believing in me, because God still had a lot of work to do in me. I soon realized that, once you have changed, other people's opinions of you don't change quite as fast. Everyone around me thought that my deciding to preach was a joke. There is no way that God would call Otis Kenner to preach the gospel! The truth is that I felt the same way. I thought, "God can't use people like me. I have issues and secrets that I've never told anyone. I am not ready yet." We sometimes try to measure God's ways by our own standards, but God doesn't see people as we see ourselves or each other. God's view is much deeper than ours. What we see as not worthy God sees as worth saving.

> Wherefore I say unto thee, her sins, which are many, are forgiven; for she loved much; but to whom little is forgiven, the same loveth little.
>
> (Luke 7:47 KJV)

The one that is forgiven the most has a much greater appreciation for having been forgiven than does one who has been forgiven for small transgressions. They recognize the indebtedness to the one who has the power to forgive them. In addition, the one who was a sinner is a greater witness to the sinner. The one who was in bondage is a greater witness to the one who is in bondage. How could you persuade someone with a message that has not persuaded you? Quoting Scripture is fine, but what people really want to know is how the Scripture you are quoting has worked for you. For example, I am bald, so it wouldn't be feasible for me to sell hair-growth products. Could you imagine my face on a product called Super Growth Formula? It just would not be convincing to a potential consumer.

The words that God spoke to me were so powerful and quick that my heart immediately began to change. I no longer wanted to live a promiscuous life, but I was not completely ready for a life of celibacy or waiting until God blessed me with a wife either. I had four relationships and hoped one would work out, but none of them did. It seemed that all I had done was coming back to me—every lie, every trick, every disappointment, every betrayal ... this was the aftermath. Once God saw that I had enough lies, tricks, disappointments and betrayals reciprocated back to me, that voice spoke again, saying, "Complete celibacy." That's when my life really took a change for the better. I completely turned away from the lifestyle of fornication: I refused telephone calls and telephone conversations with women, and I didn't go out on dates. It was the best time ever in my life. I sat for hours and talked to God, and for the first time in my life, I didn't need anyone but God to be there with me. All kinds of women were coming after me, but I refused to give up the peace and comfort of God. God and I were as one. He showed me the problems I had and why I had them. He delivered me from myself. I'd never seen myself as needing to be delivered from myself, but that was a turning point in my life.

Last, when I was the assistant pastor of a church in New Orleans pastored by Jermaine R. Hampton, my good friend and little brother who now pastors Prayer Tower Church of God In Christ, I preached a sermon titled "To Live in Christ and to Die is Gain." After the sermon was over, I sang "The Jesus in Me Loves the Jesus in You (because of That You're Easy to Love)." A young woman on the praise team, Tyra Haywood, sang along with me in the most beautiful harmony ever. While we sang that song together, the voice came to me again, soft and subtle now, saying, "That same harmony you have in that song you can have in your life." (I learned after that that when God's voice is loud and aggressive, it demonstrates warning but; when God's voice is subtle, it demonstrates direction and a level of maturity in your relationship with God. When a child is young, a parent has to show sternness to establish the authority of his or her voice, but once that authority is established, force is no longer necessary to validate the authority behind the voice. I no longer needed God to speak forcibly to me, as I understood His authority.)

I told Tyra what I had heard, and she said she needed to hear from God herself, but later she told me she had heard from God. "Are we going to get engaged?" she asked.

"No," I said, "we are going to get married." We then began spending time getting to know each other and encouraging one another by reading books that spiritually enhanced marriages. One in particular was, "Marriage Enrichment" by Bishop Andrew Merritt. Three months later we were married, and we have been married now for more than eighteen wonderful years. When God got ready, he presented me with a wife.

Even though I was married and happy, there was still a problem: the wreckage of my past. I had explained my past life to Tyra before we were married, including the truth about the children I had fathered. We felt it was important that I now go back into the wreckage and get my children in order to raise them in a God-fearing environment. The Lord gave me divine favor, as I was able to get all of my children and raise all of them in one house as one family in the Lord, regardless of how they all got here.

After eighteen years of marriage and sixteen years of pastoring, my wife walked into my study one afternoon after church service with a smile on her face and a picture in her hand of a nineteen-year-old man who looked exactly like me.

"Who is this that looks just like me?" I asked.

She replied, "Your son."

"My son?"

The young man had contacted my sister and explained to her that he was my son and that his mother had never told me about him. He had recently found out who I was and wanted to get to know me. He'd given my sister his telephone number and immediately after we left church I went to her house and called him.

When I telephoned him, I told him I wasn't sure who his mother was but that I was sure that he belonged to me. The next week I flew to Leavenworth, Kansas, to meet him at his home, where he lived with his grandmother, to sign paternity papers to give him my name. He was so excited when my taxi pulled up to his house that he ran to car, hugged and kissed me, and said, "My dad."

I was amazed at how much he looked like me. I was excited to meet him, but it was as if I'd known him all his life. We spent all night talking, and the next day we were on an airplane, and he was coming home for the very first time.

That Sunday I preached a sermon from the passage of Scripture in which King David invited Mephibosheth to the palace where Mephibosheth had once lived as the prince of the kingdom. His true identity had been lost in the shadows of Lodebar, which is a place of no pasture, lifelessness, desiccated and dry: a place of hopelessness. The sermon topic was "Going Home to Discover Who I Am." It was a beautiful day. I introduced him to the congregation as my son, and they all rejoiced with me ... the aftermath.

CHAPTER 11

Counting Up the Cost

> For which of you, intending to build a tower sitteth not down first, and counteth the cost, whether he had sufficient to finish it?
> —Luke 14:28 (KJV)

When I accepted the call into ministry, I realized that the calling was not just to salvation but to holiness as well. I knew then that my life could not remain as it was if I were to go where God was taking me. Church as I knew it then was business as usual, but I felt that God was calling me to something greater, something different. To get there would cost me everything, and the road would be difficult and sometimes lonely. Sacrifice would be a way of life for me. Every claim that I had to a private life was out of the door, as it would be no more "I" but Christ. Ministry would be something that I not only did but who I was.

I found myself questioning why we do some things in church fellowship for which I could never find a biblical reference, and when I talked to some pastors about it, they never had a legitimate answer. After seven years of going through the program of religious conformity, worn down by imposed regulations and rituals that never made the worshippers better, I became programmatic and found myself, as it relates to church, religious at the cost of relationship. There was no real sense of meaning or purpose to what I was doing; it just seemed to meet the moral criteria for that Sunday. Then God spoke to me, saying, "Remove all traditional and religious restraints, and I will unveil my Word to you." What refreshing words spoken at the time of need! Then he said, "Lead my people back to me." The Lord revealed to me that many worshippers knew religion but didn't know Christ. They had a habit of worship but didn't have the heart of worship. They had praise, but their praise was without substance. They had an external show but no internal power.

> Having a form of Godliness, but denying the power thereof: from such turn away. (2 Timothy 3:5 KJV)

The Lord also revealed that organized religions have become a form of paganism and idolatry, infiltrated by devils. He said again, "Go and lead my people back to me" and began to show me the religious injustice and bigotry that has circulated throughout the religious community for centuries.

John 4 describes a Samaritan woman with five husbands, whose current lover was not her own husband, and John 8 describes a woman caught in the act of adultery. In each of these cases, there's religious injustice and bigotry that goes unaddressed. Let's start with the Samaritan woman: The language of the Scripture suggests that she was a prostitute because, according to Leviticus 20:10, an adulteress would have been stoned to death. Verese 18 says that the lover she had was not her own husband. In biblical times, prostitution was a known and accepted occupation in the east. Even Judah, an ancestor of the Lord Jesus Christ, paid for the services of a harlot who was his daughter-in-law in disguise (Genesis 38:13–16). The Corinthian church was exposed to this problem through the worship of Aphrodite. At an acropolis elevated 1800 feet, designated as the place to worship her, a thousand temple prostitutes engaged in sexual orgies that constituted worship to Aphrodite. In Judges 16:16, Delilah was able to seduce Sampson with her sensuality because she was a cultic prostitute, and in Judges 11:1, the mother of Jephthah the Gileadite was a zonah, a common prostitute. How is it that the woman in John chapter 8 was going to be stoned to death but in John Chapter 4 was a zonah? When someone new came into the city, she would have directed them to a place to sleep where they could retain her services. It is also well established that in biblical days children were sold as a either cultic prostitutes for religious services to stimulate the gods or as zonahs for social entertainment in the city to stimulate the city's economics. John 8 describes how they brought the woman to be stoned but not the man, when the law clearly stated that both the adulterer and the adulteress should be stoned. What this demonstrates is how religiously one person's behavior is overlooked and never dealt with while another's is treated like an incurable disease. Religiously homosexuals are looked at as needing to be stoned to death, while the fornicator is not. This demonstrates religious bigotry and double standards in the church, but all unrighteousness is sin; one is not greater or lesser than the other. Sin is sin.

> Know ye not that the unrighteous shall not inherit the kingdom of God? Be not deceived: neither fornicators, nor idolaters, nor adulterers, nor effeminate, nor abusers of themselves with mankind.

Nor thieves, nor covetousness, nor drunkards, nor revilers, nor extortioners, shall inherit the kingdom of God. But such were some of you but ye are washed. (1 Corinthians 6:9–11 KJV)

The Scripture does not single out one sin above or below the others. Sin is sin. Jesus Christ died for all humankind's sin. The fornicator cannot change himself or herself. The drunkard cannot change himself or herself. The homosexual cannot change himself, and the lesbian cannot change herself. There is only one solution for the fall of man and the sin of humankind, and that is Lord Savior Jesus Christ.

When God told me to lead His people back to him, I declassified myself from any denomination as a faith, and I went in quest of God and His Word in order to know the deepest mysteries of His holy Word. I knew the voyage was going to be hard, that it wouldn't be without loss, that I would have to navigate some unchartered waters, and that disappointments would be inevitable.

When I spoke with my mother about what God was doing with me, she said, "You were born a Baptist, and you are going to die a Baptist." What my mother did not understand was that it had nothing to do with being Baptist, Catholic, Pentecostal or any other faith; it had to do with God's revealing Himself and Christ Jesus in a relationship that is real and personal. One of the first revelations I received from God was the involuntary worship of devils through the ignorance of pagan practices that have infiltrated church worship. Many of the holidays we celebrate in church have their origins in pagan practices, yet we celebrate them even after we have learned better because the world suggests that you should. In the meantime, that which God recommend for us to do goes unattended.

> But he answered and said unto them, why do ye also transgress the commandments of God by your traditions? (Matthew 15:3KJV)

> But in vain do they worship me, teaching for the doctrine the commandments of men. (Matthew 15:9 KJV)

The Pharisees were full of religion without relationship, and Jesus called them hypocrites. In many cases, when he spoke to them, he used the word *woe*.

This is the reason that, when we started our church fellowship more than sixteen years ago, I removed the holidays that had their roots in pagan customs from observance in our worship services. I knew I would receive some ridicule for it and that other preachers would turn away from me because I was not conforming to the church's religious customs, but I was willing to pay the price because I wanted to please God. After all, I was born like this.

God released the church from under the oppression of having to keep a feast day as a means of religious righteousness, so we should not allow customs and traditions to put us back under such oppression. We are complete in Christ, who is the head of the church, the body of Christ. If we cannot find these practices in the Bible more than 2100 years after the resurrection of Christ, then why do we keep them?

Another problem that I found was the celebration of religious services for auxiliary and other anniversaries and annual programs. These are not biblical practices but income streams through the spirit of false worship. People are being scammed again, as these services are not related to winning souls but to the god of money, giving praise to man, stealing glory from God, and preachers swapping pulpits to make money off the people of God.

In 2013 I became the presiding Bishop of Kingdom Growth Fellowship of United Churches. Many of the pastors pulled out because I would not support these kinds of services. I was no longer close to preachers with whom I had once been close because I would not compromise the standard of integrity in God's Word. The people deserve much more than this. I had to count up the cost, but when you take a stand for the truth, people will bail out on you, as they did to Jesus Christ, Paul, Moses, and many others. I am who God called me to be, and in being me I must count up the cost.

> To this end was I born, and for this cause came I into the world, that I should bear witness unto the truth. Every one that is of the truth heareth my voice. (John 18:37)

I was born to adversity.

CHAPTER 12

I Survived

> And, behold there came a great wind from the wilderness, and smote the four corners of the house, it fell upon the young man and killed them; and I only am left alone to tell this.
>
> —Job 1:19

When we focus on this passage of Scripture, Job seems to eclipse the other contributors, and we try to capture Job's struggle, faith, and patience. My focus in this chapter is to present the lives of the four unknown servants of Job who are mentioned in verses 15–19, around each of whom everyone died but who miraculously survived to tell their stories.

In 1992 a school psychologist from the St. Charles Parish School System, who counseled me from sixth grade into high school, came to talk with me, and what he said to me became a permanent part of my spiritual life. He told me that his psychological evaluation read that I would be either dead or in prison by the time I was twenty-one. He told me I should return to my high school, Destrehan High School, to speak to some of the students who were experiencing some of the same things that I experienced. Considering all that I'd been through—molestation, mishandling, mistakenly put in special education classes, made fun of by my peers, chased by demons—that psychological evaluation would have been right had God not intervened. Because God intervened, I survived.

Two thousand and thirteen was one of the most difficult years of my life. Things were going well in ministry, but I was attacked, as the Enemy waged war in my spiritual and financial lives. One of the ministries I founded and oversaw suffered a terrible split that caused me much hurt and disappointment. By nature, I "love hard," and it is difficult for me to let those I care about go. What made matters worse was that I was spiritually tired. I had to step up and pastor this ministry in order to restore order and give hope to those who were committed to remain.

There was a sleeper cell in the ministry that was pulling congregants out of our fellowship into another ministry, and one of my daughters cursed me to my face for the first time. My wife and I had to make a decision: Do we keep our son in college and stay in full-time ministry by mortgaging or selling our home, or do we go back to the secular workforce and give up full-time ministry? We chose to keep our son in college, stay in full-time ministry, and move back into our old home.

One day I started experiencing the symptoms of a person who had had a stroke. My speech was slurred, and my words were confused and out of context. I had been deprived of sleep and could not remember what day it was or what I'd done the day before. One day, after fellowship was over, I asked one of my daughters to tell me her name. I was confusing people I knew very well, one of whom was Dr. J. Cressend Schonberg, who had served with me on the St. Charles Community Health Center's Board of Directors for ten years. When I called him "Mr. Bob" twice in one week, he asked me if I was okay. I tried to brush it off, but I was far from being okay. I was over-stressed, unrested, and burned out. That one act of concern from Dr. Schonberg may have saved the quality of my life. I was under a spiritual attack that rendered me incapable of performing my pastoral duties. I haven't taken a true break from anything for thirty years; I have just gone from one challenging scene to the next. It was Satan's master design to render me incompetent and cause spiritual suicide, but I survived. I have always been highly committed to whatever I do and always do it to the fullest extent. Saying no has always been impossible. I had to learn to say no and to make a clear and discerning decision about where I needed to be, wanted to be, or was expected to be.

Fortunately, a couple in our ministry treated my wife and me to a vacation in Hawaii, which was much needed at the time. Little did they know what I was going through! It took eight thousand miles between me and my problems and a daily 2:30 am devotion with God to get me focused and back on track.

I believe that, no matter what illness or misfortune takes place in our lives, whether we were born into it or born with it, all of us have a survival instinct. In spite of the Adamic nature we received from Adam, Christ Jesus the Lord, who came not to condemn the world but to save the world through Him, is our new nature. As the apostle Paul said, by the grace of God, I continued unto today.

My Survival Testimonies

Not long after I was called into the ministry, and long before I was married, I slept with a woman who was HIV-positive and who had me on her "hit list." It was only by the grace of God that I did not contract the virus. I survived. I also recall chaperoning my sister's birthday party at the hall that is now our church building. I noticed a young man I'd never seen before watching my every move. I thought, "Before this night is over, he and I will fight." When I told everyone it was time to wrap things up, that young man yelled at me, using vulgar language. I threw off my coat and ran toward him, but he pulled out a 9mm handgun, pressed it to my forehead, started to pull the trigger. My brother-in-law snatched the gun out of his hand before he could finish. I later found out that the young man was from the St. Thomas Housing project in New Orleans, that he had found out that a girl had given him HIV, and that, out of anger, he was searching for someone to kill that night. By the grace of God, I survived.

When I was twelve years old, my cousin and I were hunting blackbirds at John L. Ory Elementary School in La Place, Louisiana. When my cousin pointed a high-powered pellet gun six inches from my temple, I told him that my dad said to never point a gun at a person because sometimes they just go off. My cousin responded, "Shut up, Little Otis. This gun is not going to go off." When I lifted my hands to move the gun from my head, the gun discharged, and the pellet hit my cheek bone and ricocheted. I was rushed to the hospital, and the doctor said, if the pellet had hit two centimeters higher, it would have hit the soft temple area and killed me.

I survived these near-tragic events neither because of chance nor luck but by God's divine providence. To God be the glory, I survived.

CHAPTER 13

Why Now?

For many who are reading this book, the question that comes to mind is "why now?" Why would this author want to expose his life in this manner now? After all, God has lifted him up to prominence, he's well respected by many of his contemporaries, and he's considered a God-fearing man of integrity by many ethnic groups. As it relates to the Christian community, he's anointed: a great preacher and a great teacher. Why uncover such intimate and graphic details about his life? Why is he so explicit? What is he trying to accomplish?

The answer is that it is important to God for the world to know what's behind the white robe, to unveil the presumption of the innocent childhood and young adulthood that most believe I had, and to make clear to people that preachers in white robes were not necessarily born that way. Too often people mistakenly conceive the idea that preachers have lived perfect lives since birth, when the truth is that many of us have come through many trials, tragedies, and even near-death experiences. I want the world to know what is behind this white robe and to share my life and some of its darkest hours in order to bring deliverance. It is also my sincere desire to bring awareness to both victims and the perpetrators of the consequences of the decisions they make and that social and emotional scars are not as easily removed as they are inflicted. I want to alert parents of certain behaviors that are sure signs of molestation or abuse (e.g. instability, low self-esteem, inferiority, lack of confidence, depression, sexual promiscuity and anger, even the crisis of sexual identity) in order to bring about a swift intervention before it's too late.

Somewhere in this world there are boys, girls, men, and women who are contemplating suicide because they feel as though life has been unfair and that there is no reason to continue their existence. They have been traumatized in some way and cannot see beyond today. I want to assure you that there is another day approaching that presents a new chapter for their lives. For people who have hidden tendencies or dark secrets that they are afraid to talk about in fear of what family and friends might say, suicide often becomes their way of escape. If you are one of those people, I want you to know that you are not alone. I not only sympathize but empathize with you. Your situation is not uncommon, and God is here to help you transition to a brighter life.

> There had no temptation taken you but such as is common to man: But God is faithful, who will not suffer you to be tempted above that ye are able; but will with the temptation also make a way to escape that you may be able to bear it. (1 Corinthians 10:13)

"Why now?" you ask. Many people have been held captive in their consciences because of a decision they made for which they find it difficult to forgive themselves. I want to present the keys of the kingdom that Jesus has delivered unto me whereby you can unlock the gate, let yourself out, and begin to enjoy life.

Why now? Somewhere in this world, there's a young woman who is feeling the need to step into adulthood and give birth to a child as a way to reverse the hidden tragedy of the child within herself that is in a psychotic state. That young woman feels the need to protect this unborn child from the life from which she herself was not protected, when the truth is that she just needs someone to talk to so she has time to heal her wounds.

Why now? I knew a person some years ago who said some things about me that were not true. I was extremely offended by it, but later I heard that he and his wife had been having problems. Even so, when I ran into him at a local grocery store and he tried to start a conversation, because of how I felt about what he did, I was short with him. My thought was to hold him at arm's length to protect myself. Two weeks later he killed his wife and himself. I cried desperately when I received the news and asked myself over and over how I could be so stupid as to miss an opportunity to minister to someone in such need. I was supposed to help people change their lives. I don't want another opportunity to change or save someone else's life to pass me by.

When God began to press me to write this book, I became a running faucet of sorts, a conduit of information to reach out to anyone who is hurting and injured. I knew then that, if I were to write the book, I would have to pull out all the stops and get down to the truth. At this point, it doesn't matter what people may think of me. I want to reach lifeless and injured people who may be about to give up.

I asked God, "Why me, Lord? Why did I have to live through this?"

His response was, "You needed a platform for your ministry so that, when you preach, you can do it from the very core of your being and empathize with people in such an intense way that, when they hear the word, they not only hear what you say but they also see what you say and experience every moment in real time." Jesus Christ bought the rights to me over two thousand years ago and allowed me to come into this world for a purpose. I am in hot pursuit of that purpose such that, by me through Christ, someone will find the help he or she needs and enjoy life as God has intended them to do so. That's why!